I0104738

Organizational Courage Assessment

RALPH H. KILMANN
LINDA A. O'HARA
JUDY P. STRAUSS

Copyright © 2002 to 2011 by Organizational Design Consultants (ODC). All rights reserved. This material may not be reproduced, stored in a retrieval system, or transmitted in any form by any means—electronic, mechanical, photocopying, video recording, or otherwise—without the prior written permission from ODC. Contact: ralph@kilmann.com.

Distributed by
KILMANN DIAGNOSTICS
1 Suprema Drive
Newport Coast, CA 92657
www.kilmanndiagnostics.com
info@kilmanndiagnostics.com
949.497.8766

ORGANIZATIONAL COURAGE ASSESSMENT

Introduction

For organizations to succeed in the short term, members must do what is required: perform their jobs, follow the standard operating procedures, and respect the decisions of their managers. But to succeed in the long term, it may be necessary for members to challenge traditional practices, confront their managers and co-workers, and bypass official policies and procedures—even though members may receive negative consequences (such as ridicule, criticism, reprimands, negative performance reviews, or even the loss of their job) for not following the organization's accepted ways of doing things.

This instrument reveals twenty *possible acts of courage* that go beyond what is safe and customary. You are asked to respond to these twenty acts in two different ways. First, you are asked to indicate how often you have *observed* these acts in your organization—or if any of these acts are not necessary because the members have already been doing what is needed for the long-term survival and success of your organization. Second, for these same possible acts of courage, you are asked to indicate how *afraid* people would be of receiving negative consequences if they performed these acts in your organization.

COPYRIGHT © 2002–2011 BY ORGANIZATIONAL DESIGN CONSULTANTS. ALL RIGHTS RESERVED.

ORGANIZATIONAL COURAGE ASSESSMENT

Part I
Instructions

Below you will find twenty possible acts of courage that can take place in an organization. For each item, circle the number that best captures how often you have observed this act inside your organization or work unit: ranging from *0, Never Observed,* to *4, Regularly Observed....* However, **if this act is not needed** in your organization because people are already doing what is necessary for the long-term success of their organization and the well-being of its members, circle **4, ...Not Needed**, the identical number as *Regularly Observed....* Circle only one number for each item, even if the response categories are difficult to distinguish at times.

		Never Observed	Rarely	Occasionally	Often	Regularly Observed or Not Needed
1.	I have observed people coming to another's aid when that person was being unfairly treated or ridiculed.	0	1	2	3	4
2.	I have observed people taking the time to say what they really think in a group meeting, even when managers were in a hurry to make a decision.	0	1	2	3	4
3.	I have observed people speaking out against illegal or unethical actions.	0	1	2	3	4
4.	I have observed people standing up for what they believe in when it was not the majority view.	0	1	2	3	4

COPYRIGHT © 2002–2011 BY ORGANIZATIONAL DESIGN CONSULTANTS. ALL RIGHTS RESERVED.

ORGANIZATIONAL COURAGE ASSESSMENT

		Never Observed	Rarely	Occasionally	Often	Regularly Observed or Not Needed

5. I have observed people speaking out if another person was harmed because of discrimination.

        0   *1*   *2*   *3*   *4*

6. I have observed people telling a boss they would not put up with his/her abusive actions that were harmful to other employees.

        0   *1*   *2*   *3*   *4*

7. I have observed people proposing an idea because they believed it was right, even when they knew it would probably be rejected sometime later.

        0   *1*   *2*   *3*   *4*

8. I have observed people publicly admitting a personal shortcoming in themselves in order to improve their work relationships.

        0   *1*   *2*   *3*   *4*

9. I have observed people not following supervisors' orders when those orders compromised ethical or moral principles.

        0   *1*   *2*   *3*   *4*

10. I have observed people standing up for fellow employees who were not being treated appropriately.

        0   *1*   *2*   *3*   *4*

COPYRIGHT © 2002–2011 BY ORGANIZATIONAL DESIGN CONSULTANTS. ALL RIGHTS RESERVED.

ORGANIZATIONAL COURAGE ASSESSMENT

	Never Observed	Rarely	Occasionally	Often	Regularly Observed or Not Needed

11. I have observed people admitting their mistakes to their superiors.

    0   1   2   3   4

12. I have observed women or minority group members speaking out to defend their points of view in white, male-dominated groups.

    0   1   2   3   4

13. I have observed people going beyond the limits of their authority to fix a problem for a customer.

    0   1   2   3   4

14. I have observed people telling their managers that someone was being treated unfairly.

    0   1   2   3   4

15. I have observed people refusing an assignment that involved doing something ethically or morally wrong.

    0   1   2   3   4

16. I have observed people fighting to hire someone over others' objections, because they believed that individual was the best person for the job.

    0   1   2   3   4

COPYRIGHT © 2002-2011 BY ORGANIZATIONAL DESIGN CONSULTANTS. ALL RIGHTS RESERVED.

ORGANIZATIONAL COURAGE ASSESSMENT

	Never Observed	Rarely	Occasionally	Often	Regularly Observed or Not Needed
17. I have observed people not following standard operating procedures in order to do something that benefits the organization.	0	1	2	3	4
18. I have observed people telling managers about the negative impact the managers were having on others.	0	1	2	3	4
19. I have observed people revealing that they were actively involved in their own personal growth in order to improve their relationships.	0	1	2	3	4
20. I have observed people accepting responsibility for something negative that they could have simply kept to themselves.	0	1	2	3	4

COPYRIGHT © 2002–2011 BY ORGANIZATIONAL DESIGN CONSULTANTS. ALL RIGHTS RESERVED.

Part II
Instructions

Below you will find the same twenty acts—looked at in a different way. This time, for each item, circle the number that best captures how *afraid* people would be of receiving negative consequences if they performed the act in your organization. Even if the response categories (0 to 4) are difficult to distinguish at times, circle the single number that is closest to your experience.

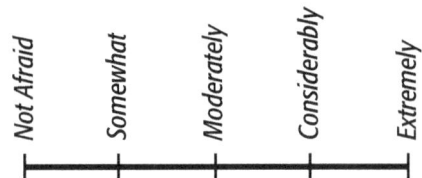

	Not Afraid	Somewhat	Moderately	Considerably	Extremely
21. How afraid would people be of coming to another's aid when that person was being unfairly treated or ridiculed?	0	1	2	3	4
22. How afraid would people be of taking the time to say what they really think in a group meeting, even when managers were in a hurry to make a decision?	0	1	2	3	4
23. How afraid would people be of speaking out against illegal or unethical actions?	0	1	2	3	4
24. How afraid would people be of standing up for what they believe in when it was not the majority view?	0	1	2	3	4

COPYRIGHT © 2002–2011 BY ORGANIZATIONAL DESIGN CONSULTANTS. ALL RIGHTS RESERVED.

	Not Afraid	Somewhat	Moderately	Considerably	Extremely
25. How afraid would people be of speaking out if another person was harmed because of discrimination?	0	1	2	3	4
26. How afraid would people be of telling a boss they would not put up with his/her abusive actions that were harmful to other employees?	0	1	2	3	4
27. How afraid would people be of proposing an idea because they believed it was right, even when they knew it would probably be rejected sometime later?	0	1	2	3	4
28. How afraid would people be of publicly admitting a personal shortcoming in themselves in order to improve their work relationships?	0	1	2	3	4
29. How afraid would people be of not following supervisors' orders when those orders compromised ethical or moral principles?	0	1	2	3	4

COPYRIGHT © 2002–2011 BY ORGANIZATIONAL DESIGN CONSULTANTS. ALL RIGHTS RESERVED.

		Not Afraid	Somewhat	Moderately	Considerably	Extremely
30.	How afraid would people be of standing up for fellow employees who were not being treated appropriately?	0	1	2	3	4
31.	How afraid would people be of admitting their mistakes to their superiors?	0	1	2	3	4
32.	How afraid would women or minority group members be of speaking out to defend their points of view in white, male-dominated groups?	0	1	2	3	4
33.	How afraid would people be of going beyond the limits of their authority to fix a problem for a customer?	0	1	2	3	4
34.	How afraid would people be of telling their managers that someone was being treated unfairly?	0	1	2	3	4
35.	How afraid would people be of refusing an assignment that involved doing something ethically or morally wrong?	0	1	2	3	4

COPYRIGHT © 2002–2011 BY ORGANIZATIONAL DESIGN CONSULTANTS. ALL RIGHTS RESERVED.

	Not Afraid	Somewhat	Moderately	Considerably	Extremely

36. How afraid would people be of fighting to hire someone over others' objections, because they believed that individual was the best person for the job?

0 1 2 3 4

37. How afraid would people be of not following standard operating procedures in order to do something that benefits the organization?

0 1 2 3 4

38. How afraid would people be of telling managers about the negative impact the managers were having on others?

0 1 2 3 4

39. How afraid would people be of revealing that they were actively involved in their own personal growth in order to improve their relationships?

0 1 2 3 4

40. How afraid would people be of accepting responsibility for something negative that they could have simply kept to themselves?

0 1 2 3 4

COPYRIGHT © 2002–2011 BY ORGANIZATIONAL DESIGN CONSULTANTS. ALL RIGHTS RESERVED.

Scoring Your Responses

In the spaces below, please transfer all the numbers that you circled on the previous pages. Then add up the columns as shown. The resulting two sums are your scores for two ingredients of organizational courage—**Observed** *Frequency of Possible Acts of Courage* and **Fear** *of Performing Possible Acts of Courage*—which will be explained shortly.

Part I		**Part II**	
1. ___	11. ___	21. ___	31. ___
2. ___	12. ___	22. ___	32. ___
3. ___	13. ___	23. ___	33. ___
4. ___	14. ___	24. ___	34. ___
5. ___	15. ___	25. ___	35. ___
6. ___	16. ___	26. ___	36. ___
7. ___	17. ___	27. ___	37. ___
8. ___	18. ___	28. ___	38. ___
9. ___	19. ___	29. ___	39. ___
10. ___	20. ___	30. ___	40. ___

[___] **+** [___] **=** [Observe Score]   [___] **+** [___] **=** [Fear Score]

COPYRIGHT © 2002–2011 BY ORGANIZATIONAL DESIGN CONSULTANTS. ALL RIGHTS RESERVED.

Graphing Your Scores

On the graph below, transfer your **Observe Score** to the top box and your **Fear Score** to the box on the right side of the page. On each axis, ranging from 0 to 80, draw a dot (or mark an X) to represent each score. Then use a large dot to mark the point on the graph where your two scores meet. This point identifies one of four possible types of organizations (or, if you scored in the middle of a scale, mixtures of these types of organizations).

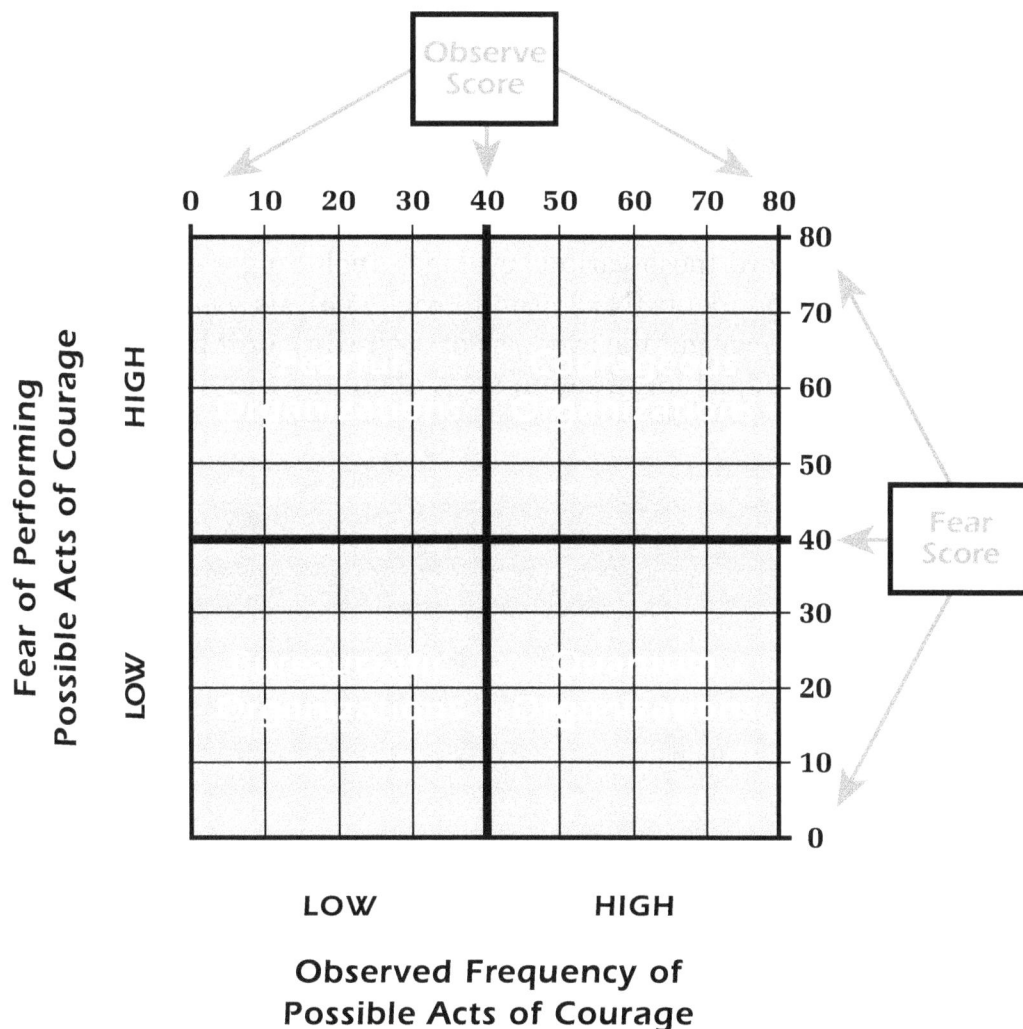

Observe Score

0 10 20 30 40 50 60 70 80

80
70
60
50
40
30
20
10
0

Fear Score

Fear of Performing Possible Acts of Courage

HIGH

LOW

LOW   HIGH

Observed Frequency of Possible Acts of Courage

COPYRIGHT © 2002–2011 BY ORGANIZATIONAL DESIGN CONSULTANTS. ALL RIGHTS RESERVED.

Calculating Average Scores

When members in your work group have calculated both *courage scores,* the **Observe Score** and **Fear Score,** collect all these numbers together on a separate sheet of paper and then calculate ***the two average courage scores*** for your work group. Be certain to divide the sum of the scores by the right number of people in your group: those who actually provided their scores for these calculations.

When the two courage scores have been averaged for your work group, enter the results in the two designated spaces on the following page for **My Work Group**. If you also have access to the other work groups in your department, you can also calculate the averages for **My Department**. And if you have access to all the departments in your organization, you can calculate the two averages for **My Organization**. On the next pages, graphs are provided to record these various averages, including a space to enter the number of respondents (N =) used in each analysis. *Note:* You might find it necessary to weight the averages of each work unit by the number of its members to adjust for different sizes of groups and departments in your organization.

COPYRIGHT © 2002–2011 BY ORGANIZATIONAL DESIGN CONSULTANTS. ALL RIGHTS RESERVED.

ORGANIZATIONAL COURAGE ASSESSMENT

Average Scores for My
WORK GROUP
N = _____

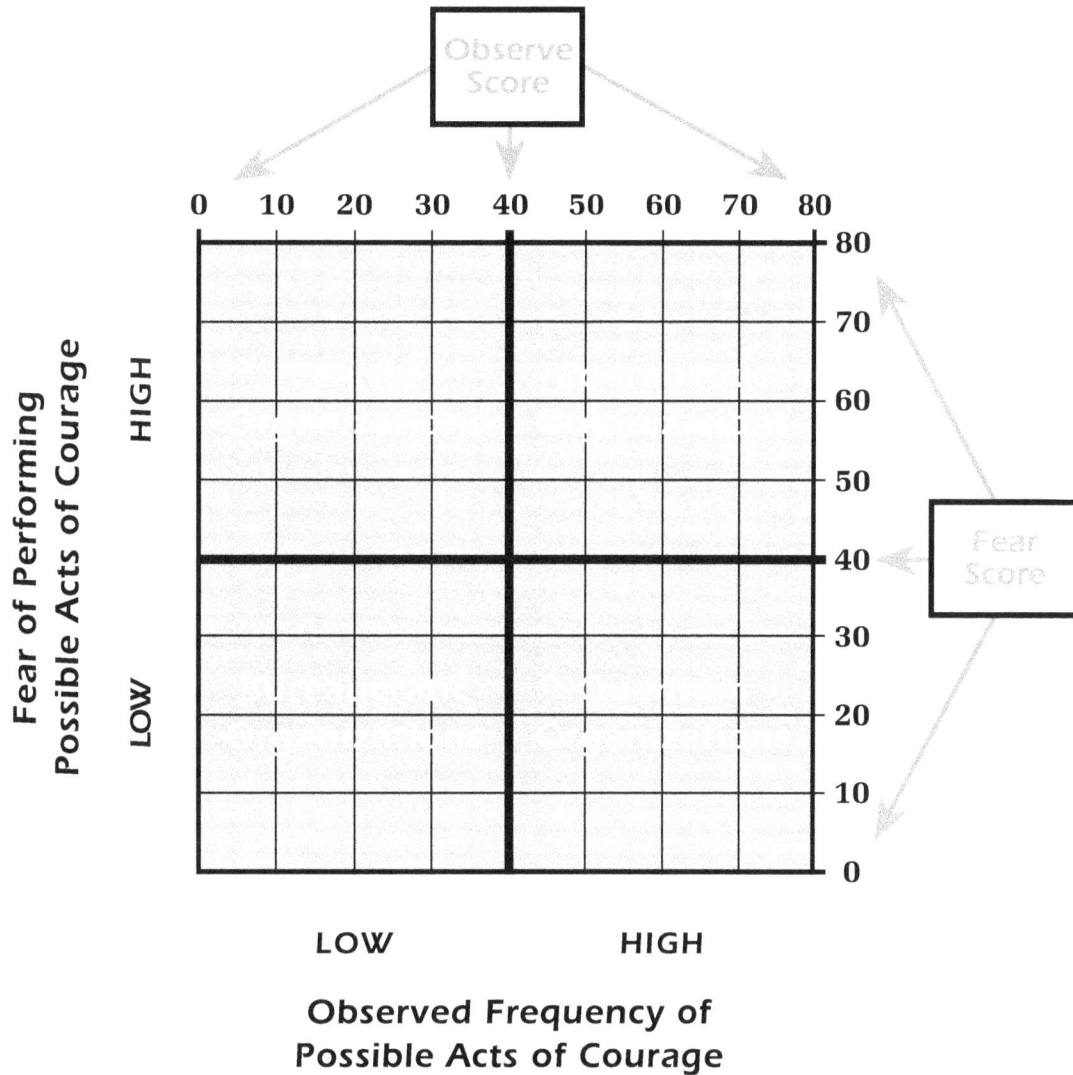

Observe Score

Fear Score

Fear of Performing
Possible Acts of Courage

HIGH

LOW

0 10 20 30 40 50 60 70 80

LOW   HIGH

Observed Frequency of
Possible Acts of Courage

COPYRIGHT © 2002–2011 BY ORGANIZATIONAL DESIGN CONSULTANTS. ALL RIGHTS RESERVED.

ORGANIZATIONAL COURAGE ASSESSMENT

Average Scores for My
DEPARTMENT
N = _____

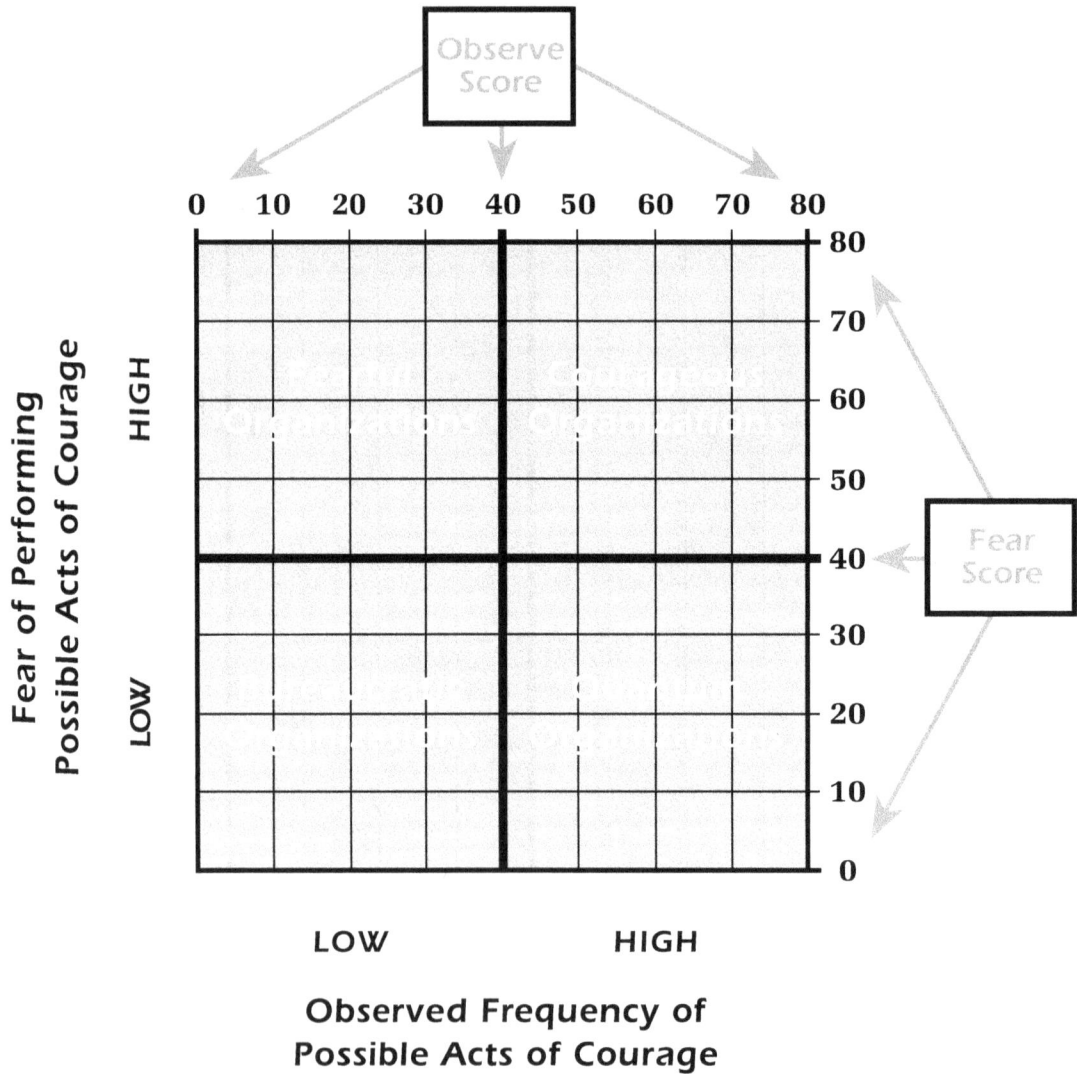

Observe
Score

Fear
Score

0   10   20   30   40   50   60   70   80

80
70
60
50
40
30
20
10
0

HIGH

LOW

Fear of Performing
Possible Acts of Courage

LOW   HIGH

Observed Frequency of
Possible Acts of Courage

COPYRIGHT © 2002–2011 BY ORGANIZATIONAL DESIGN CONSULTANTS. ALL RIGHTS RESERVED.

ORGANIZATIONAL COURAGE ASSESSMENT

Average Scores for My
ORGANIZATION
N = _____

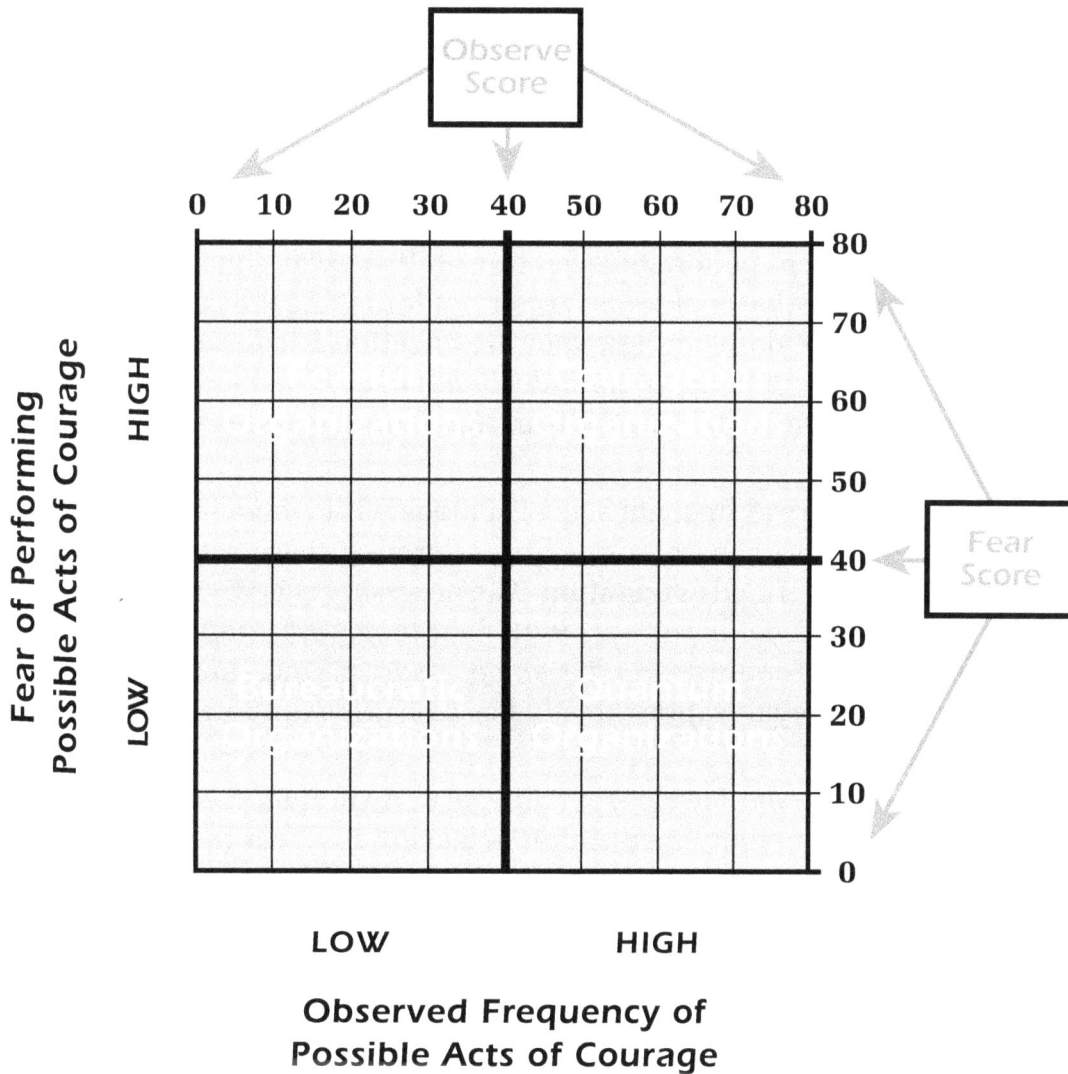

COPYRIGHT © 2002–2011 BY ORGANIZATIONAL DESIGN CONSULTANTS. ALL RIGHTS RESERVED.

Defining Four Types of Organizations

Now that you have graphed your two *courage scores* (and also graphed the average scores for your work group, department, and organization), let's define four types of organizations that are possible: (1) Courageous Organizations, (2) Quantum Organizations, (3) Fearful Organizations, and (4) Bureaucratic Organizations—as shown on the opposite page. Of course, if either of your *courage scores* is near the midpoint (40) of the scale, your organization is a mixture of these different types.

If you have observed frequent acts of courage in your organization and yet these acts were performed even though there was considerable fear of receiving negative consequences for not following the organization's accepted ways of doing things, your organization is **courageous**. Thus, the *possible* acts of courage are indeed *actual* acts of courage, because they were performed despite the fear: *the defining quality of courage.*

If you have observed frequent acts of courage while there is little fear of receiving negative consequences for performing these acts, then your organization is defined as **quantum**. The necessary acts were performed, but members did not have to act with fear: *they were supported!* Better yet, *many acts of courage aren't even necessary* because being quantum means that the organization already has a healthy/supportive culture.

If you have observed few acts of courage, and yet there is considerable fear present, then your organization is **fearful**. It is fear that is keeping members from doing what needs to be done for the long-term success of their organization and their own psychological well-being. Unless this fear is removed, members may continue doing what is required by the organization for short-term survival, but long-term success is at risk.

If you have observed few acts of courage and do not experience the fear of receiving negative consequences, your organization is **bureaucratic**. Apparently, members have resigned themselves to doing only what is officially and clearly outlined in their jobs; members are doing what is expected. Fear is not felt when people have given up trying to improve "the system." Sadly, no one is fighting for the organization's future.

COPYRIGHT © 2002–2011 BY ORGANIZATIONAL DESIGN CONSULTANTS. ALL RIGHTS RESERVED.

FOUR TYPES
OF
ORGANIZATIONS

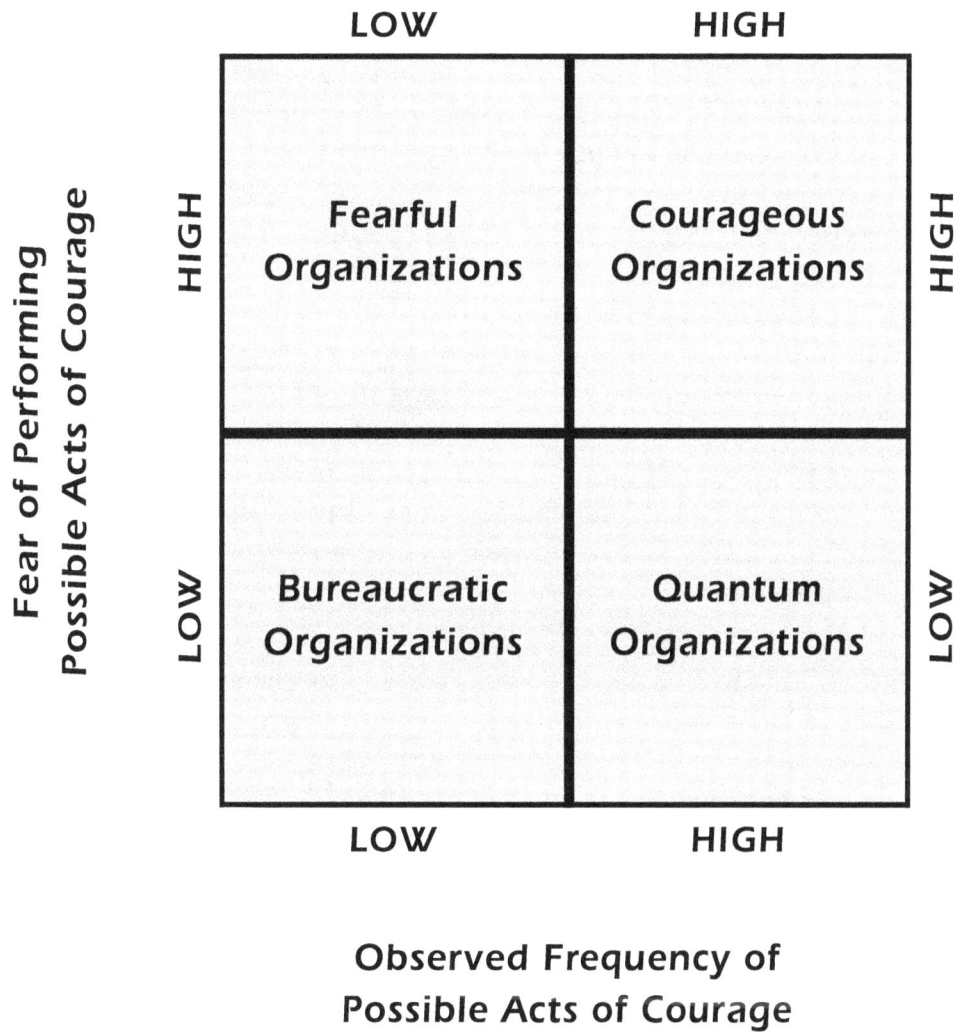

	LOW	HIGH
HIGH	Fearful Organizations	Courageous Organizations
LOW	Bureaucratic Organizations	Quantum Organizations
	LOW	HIGH

Fear of Performing Possible Acts of Courage (left axis)

Observed Frequency of Possible Acts of Courage

COPYRIGHT © 2002–2011 BY ORGANIZATIONAL DESIGN CONSULTANTS. ALL RIGHTS RESERVED.

Interpreting Your Results: Three Examples

When work group, department, and organizational averages have been calculated and graphed, it is easy to pinpoint directions for change that will improve the success of the organization as well as the psychological well-being of its members. Three examples (with graphs) are provided on the next several pages.

The opposite page illustrates the averages for an organization as a whole. Here the graph shows a **Fearful Organization**, in which members do not provide the acts of courage that are necessary—because members may be afraid of receiving negative consequences. Both the organization and its members thereby lose: The organization is not doing what is in the best interests of its customers because, in all likelihood, it is thwarted by old management practices, outdated procedures and job descriptions, and a dysfunctional culture. Indeed, this culture might be perpetuating fear— thereby members feel intimidated, cautious, and defensive about trying to do what customers really want. If the current situation is allowed to persist, the organization will gradually lose its customer base (especially in a competitive industry). Moreover, the organization may also lose its best people, who eventually leave to take jobs in a more satisfying—and successful—organization.

One alternative, however, is for the organization to accept its problems and discuss the results and implications of the *Courage Assessment.* By finding ways to enable members to take the necessary chances to do the right thing for their stakeholders *and themselves,* despite the fears that may be reinforced by an unhealthy culture, the organization will become more courageous. This **personal transformation** in members' behavior will be evident with another administration of the *Courage Assessment.*

COPYRIGHT © 2002–2011 BY ORGANIZATIONAL DESIGN CONSULTANTS. ALL RIGHTS RESERVED.

ORGANIZATIONAL COURAGE ASSESSMENT

Average Scores for My
ORGANIZATION
N = 750

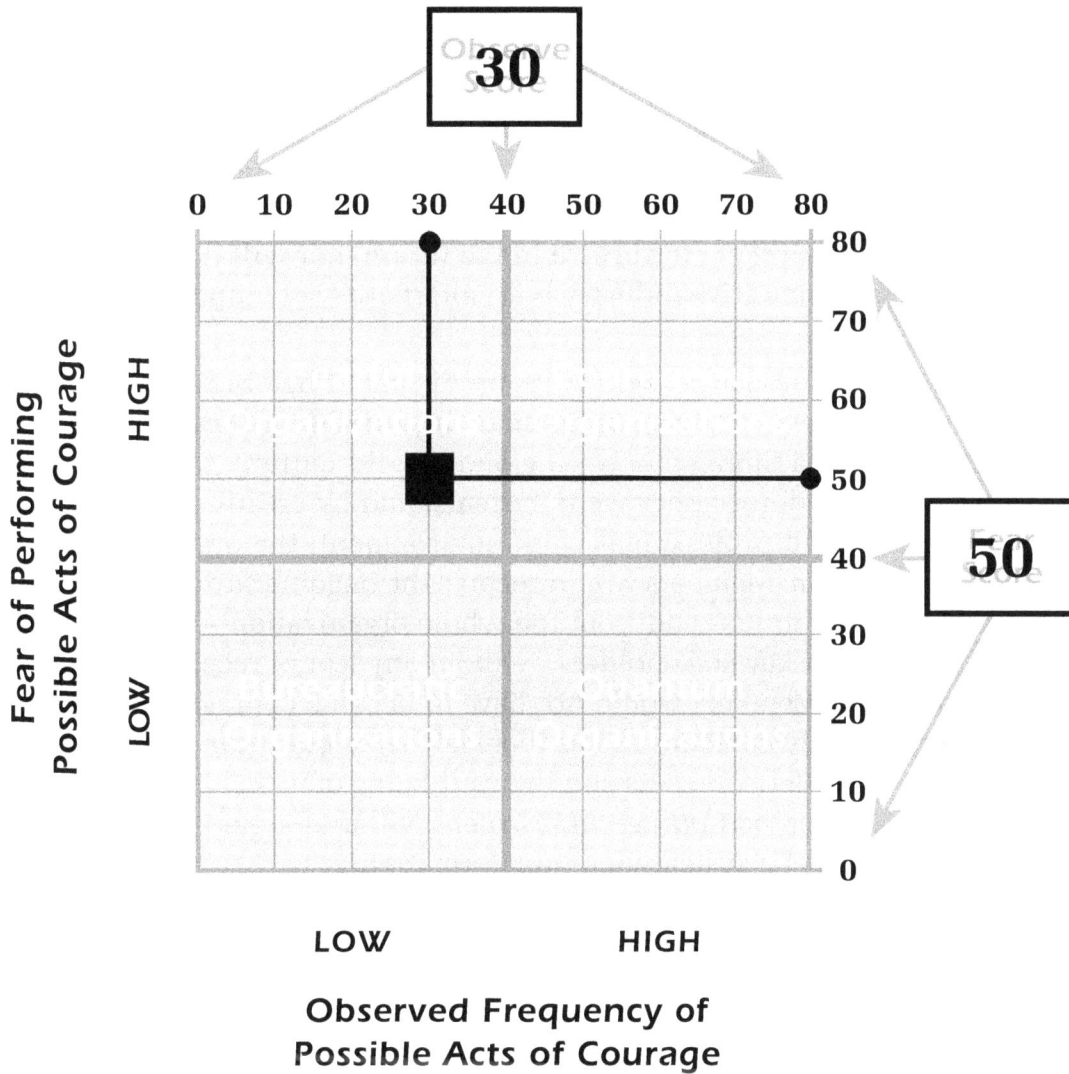

LOW   HIGH

**Observed Frequency of
Possible Acts of Courage**

COPYRIGHT © 2002–2011 BY ORGANIZATIONAL DESIGN CONSULTANTS. ALL RIGHTS RESERVED.

The opposite page provides a second, but different, illustration. Here the results point to a **Bureaucratic Organization,** in which members do not provide the necessary acts of courage *and they are not afraid of receiving negative consequences.* Essentially, the members have given up on the organization. They are not afraid to act—since they don't even consider taking chances! Not only is this organization rooted in bureaucratic red tape and out-of-date operating procedures, but its long-standing reward system along with a dysfunctional culture have also convinced members to do only the bare minimum to remain employed. Not surprisingly, this organization is unlikely to survive in the future (nor will it retain its best people) in a competitive industry with alternative job opportunities.

If the organization can recognize its predicament before it is too late, it can embark on a systemwide program of **organizational transformation.** By establishing a more empowering and candid culture, by redesigning its formal procedures and reward systems, and by creating an engaging, participative, and professional work environment, the organization can become *quantum.* Members would receive the ongoing support they need from their work units—and from the whole organization—in order to do the best for their key stakeholders, without any fear of receiving negative consequences. Members would not have to become courageous, as such, in order to satisfy customers (and themselves): a **quantum organization** ensures its long-term success and the well-being of its members. Another administration of the *Courage Assessment* will undoubtedly confirm the positive results of a systemwide transformation.

COPYRIGHT © 2002–2011 BY ORGANIZATIONAL DESIGN CONSULTANTS. ALL RIGHTS RESERVED.

Average Scores for My
ORGANIZATION
N = 825

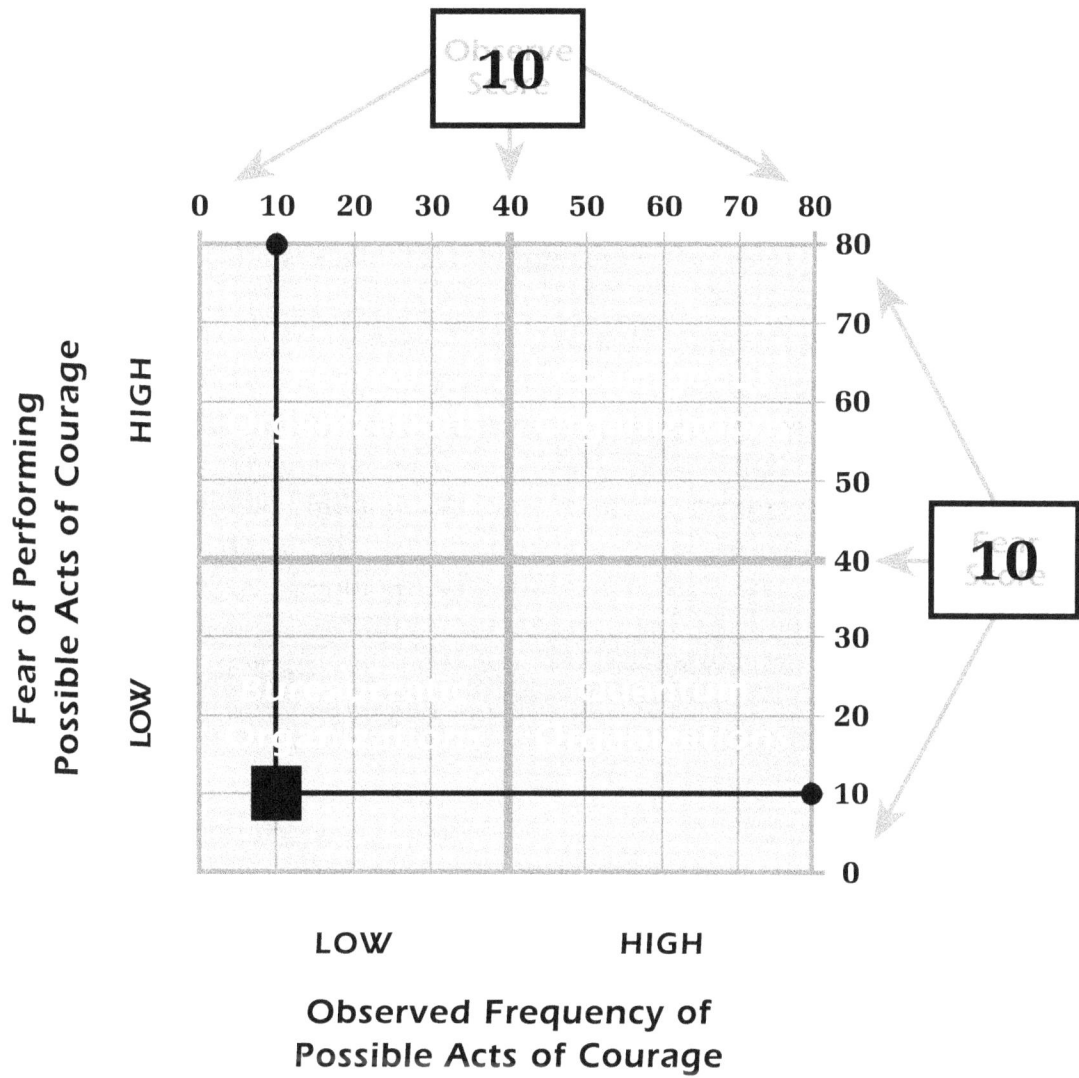

Observed Frequency of
Possible Acts of Courage

COPYRIGHT © 2002–2011 BY ORGANIZATIONAL DESIGN CONSULTANTS. ALL RIGHTS RESERVED.

The graph on the opposite page offers the third example for interpreting the results of the *Courage Assessment*. Here the average scores reveal a **Courageous Organization**, in which members perform the essential acts of courage *even though they are afraid of receiving negative consequences.* Although performing these acts of courage ensures the long-term success of the organization, it does so at a considerable price: All the enthusiasm and talent that the members can bring to the workplace are being drained by their having to overcome fear on a regular basis. Ultimately, members will have less energy available to use for productive ends; they may also get burned out if they must continually fight "the system."

Although members being courageous and also being part of a Courageous Organization are both desirable, there is a much better alternative—*if a systemwide transformation to a Quantum Organization is implemented.* By conducting a change program for renewing the organization's culture, skills, teams, strategy-structures, reward systems, and business processes, a *Courageous* Organization can thus become a **Quantum Organization**. Now members can do what is essential for the long-term success of their organization without having to live with—and overcome—fear. Both the informal and formal systems of the organization will be in sync with the needs of all internal and external stakeholders: the defining quality of a Quantum Organization.

Note: For the latest theories and methods for transforming bureaucratic, fearful, and courageous organizations into quantum organizations (also involving a personal transformation of all members), see: Kilmann, R. H., *Quantum Organizations: A New Paradigm for Achieving Organizational Success and Personal Meaning* (Newport Coast, CA: Organizational Design Consultants and Kilmann Diagnostics, 2010, 2011).

COPYRIGHT © 2002–2011 BY ORGANIZATIONAL DESIGN CONSULTANTS. ALL RIGHTS RESERVED.

ORGANIZATIONAL COURAGE ASSESSMENT

Average Scores for My
ORGANIZATION
N = 455

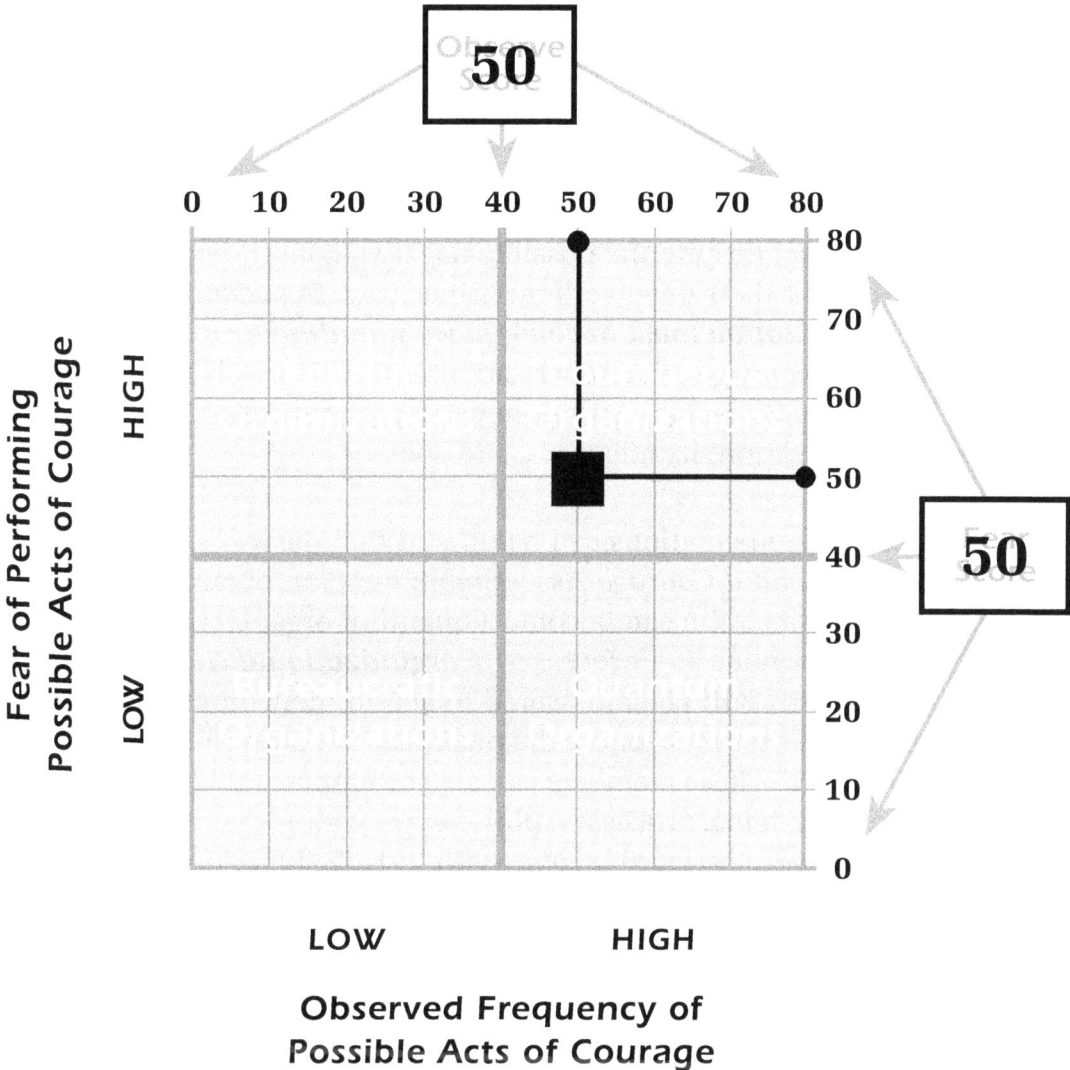

Observed Score: **50**

Fear Score: **50**

Vertical axis: **Fear of Performing Possible Acts of Courage** — HIGH / LOW, scale 0 to 80

Horizontal axis (top): 0 10 20 30 40 50 60 70 80

Horizontal axis (bottom): LOW / HIGH

Observed Frequency of Possible Acts of Courage

COPYRIGHT © 2002–2011 BY ORGANIZATIONAL DESIGN CONSULTANTS. ALL RIGHTS RESERVED.

Transforming Organizations and People

All organizations are enmeshed in an increasingly dynamic, competitive environment. It is difficult if not impossible, therefore, to specify exactly what is required of every member on a daily basis. As a result, traditional practices and standard operating procedures are no longer sufficient to guide work behavior. People must internalize what behaviors are best for the short-run as well as the long-run success of their organization—and perform these acts as needed. Hopefully, the organization will support—empower—its members to act mindfully and appropriately. However, in those cases when an organization remains entrenched with bureaucracy, members must act despite the possible negative consequences for taking responsibility for their organization. Either way, **to succeed in the long term, an organization must become more quantum or its people must act with more courage**. The other sad alternatives involve (1) members living in fear and (2) resigning their hopes for the future—either of which hurts the organization, its members, and society.

Two action recommendations can be offered that derive from the results of the *Organizational Courage Assessment*: First, an organization that is assessed as bureaucratic can become a quantum organization—applying the available programs and processes of **organizational transformation**. Thereby, members will be empowered to act on their internalized sense of what is in the best interests of the organization, both in the short term and the long term. These members can also be empowered to reinvent the organization's systems, processes, policies, procedures, and management practices in order to be more in sync with today's dynamic world.

If an organizational transformation is just not feasible, then the members in either a bureaucratic or fearful organization will have to become more courageous: to do what is needed for long-term success despite the risks of receiving negative consequences for challenging traditional practices, confronting their managers and co-workers, and ignoring official policies and procedures. Without performing the necessary acts of courage in a fearful organization (or in a bureaucratic organization), and thus without a **personal transformation** of the members, the danger arises of people living with fear or, worse yet, giving up all hope for the future.

COPYRIGHT © 2002–2011 BY ORGANIZATIONAL DESIGN CONSULTANTS. ALL RIGHTS RESERVED.

Assessment Tools for the Eight Tracks
Distributed by Kilmann Diagnostics

Kilmann-Saxton Culture-Gap® Survey

Kilmanns Organizational Belief Survey

Kilmanns Time-Gap Survey

Kilmanns Team-Gap Survey

Organizational Courage Assessment

Kilmann-Covin Organizational Influence Survey

Plus the Online Version of the

Thomas-Kilmann Conflict Mode Instrument

Plus These Training and Development Tools

Work Sheets for Identifying and Closing Culture-Gaps

Work Sheets for Identifying and Closing Team-Gaps

And the Book That Fully Explains the Eight Tracks

Quantum Organizations

www.ingramcontent.com/pod-product-compliance
Lightning Source LLC
Chambersburg PA
CBHW081205270326
41930CB00014B/3312